MW01533760

Geisha Garden Coloring Book

30 Japanese Women & Nature Scenes For Adults and Grown up Children

Rachel Mintz

Images used under license from Shutterstock.com

Copyright © 2018 Palm Tree Publishing - All rights reserved.
No part of this publication may be reproduced, distributed, or transmitted in any form or by any means, including photocopying, recording, or other electronic or mechanical methods, without the prior written permission of the publisher, except in the case of brief quotations embodied in critical reviews and certain other noncommercial uses permitted by copyright law.

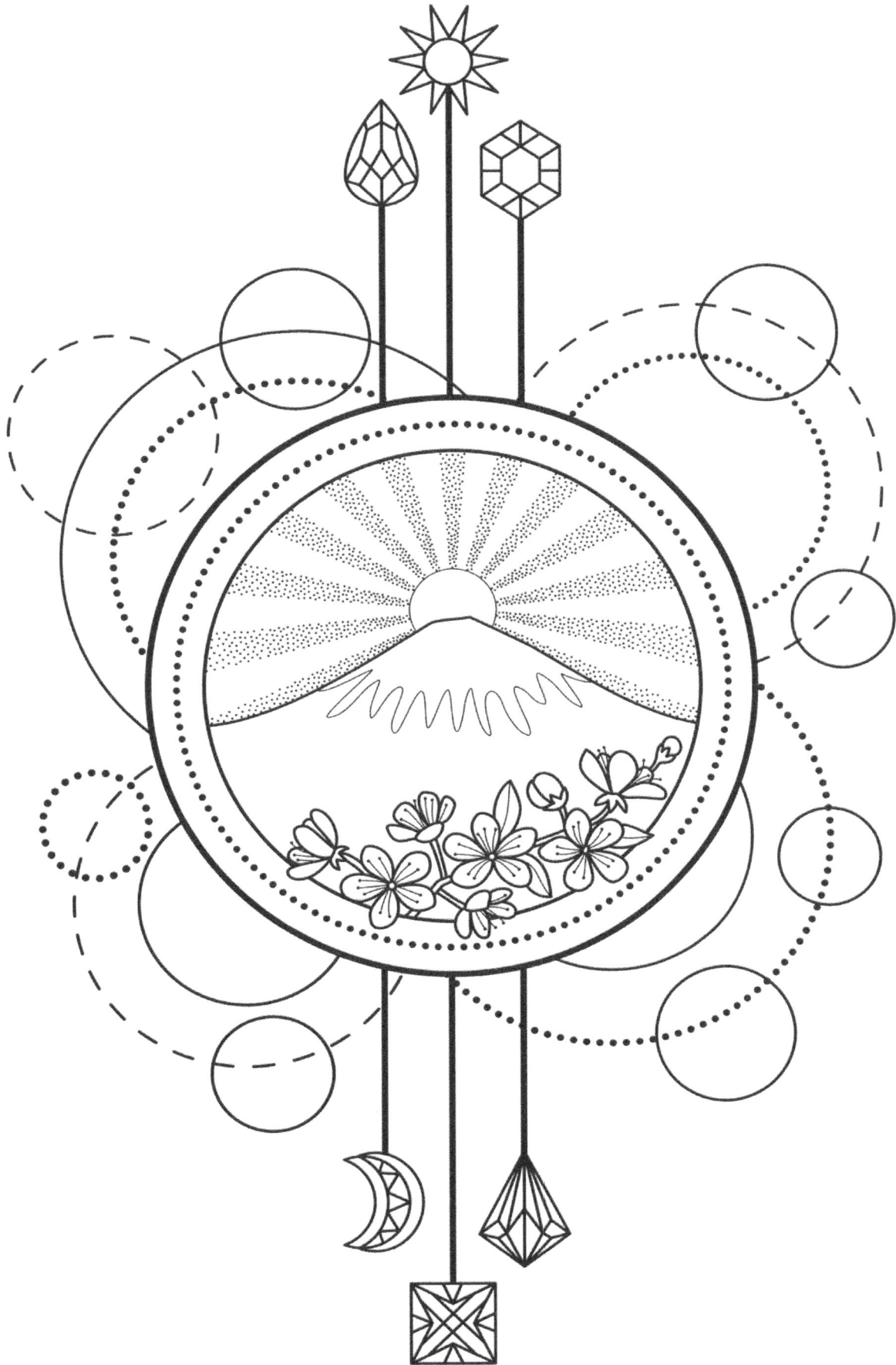

Thank you for coloring with us!

Enjoy some more of our coloring books for adults:

THE SEA OF
TRANQUILITY

Coral Reef & Marine Life Relaxing Coloring Book For Adults

Rachel Mintz

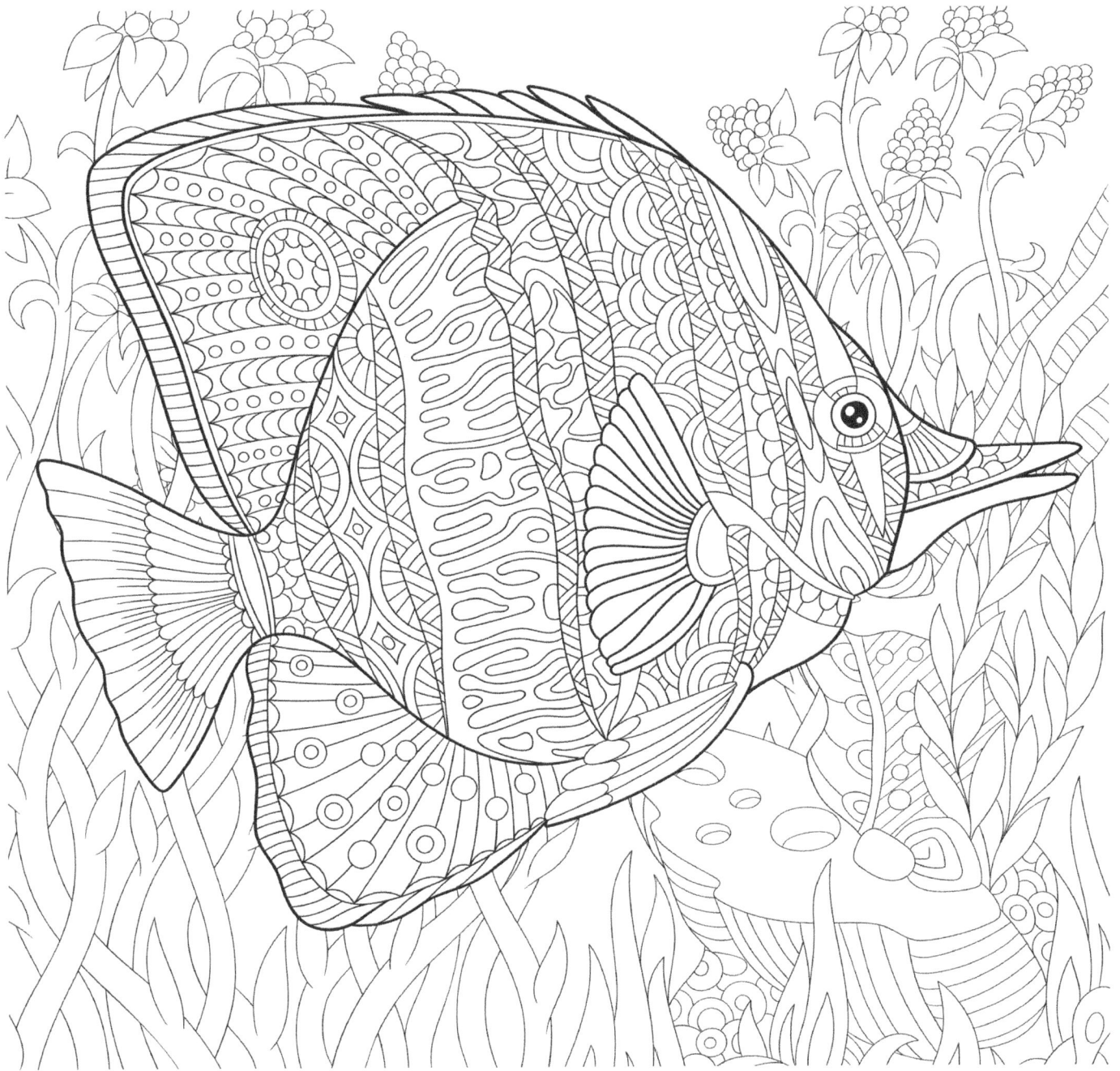

SEA

Get one more doodle designs coloring book!

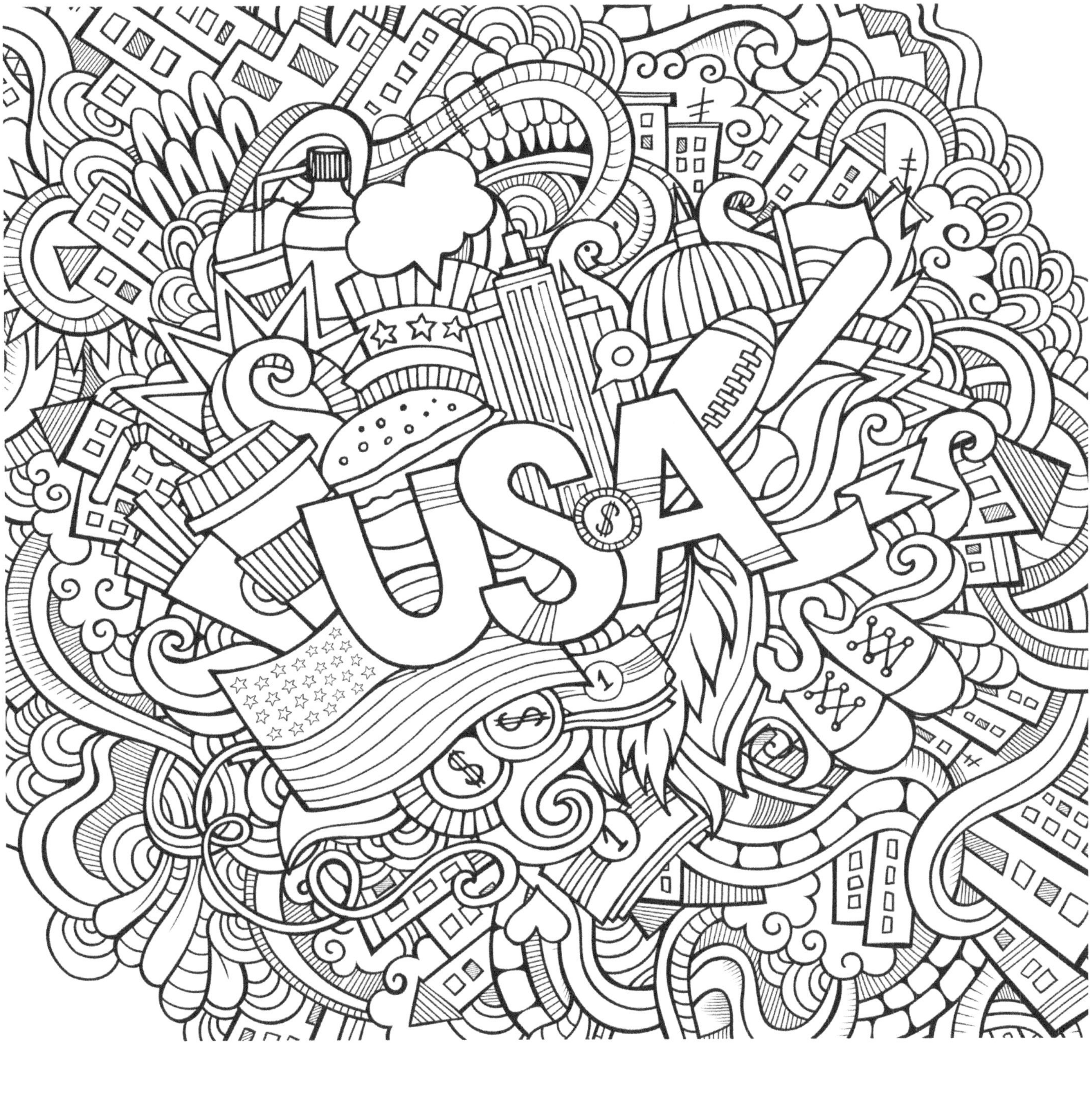
USA

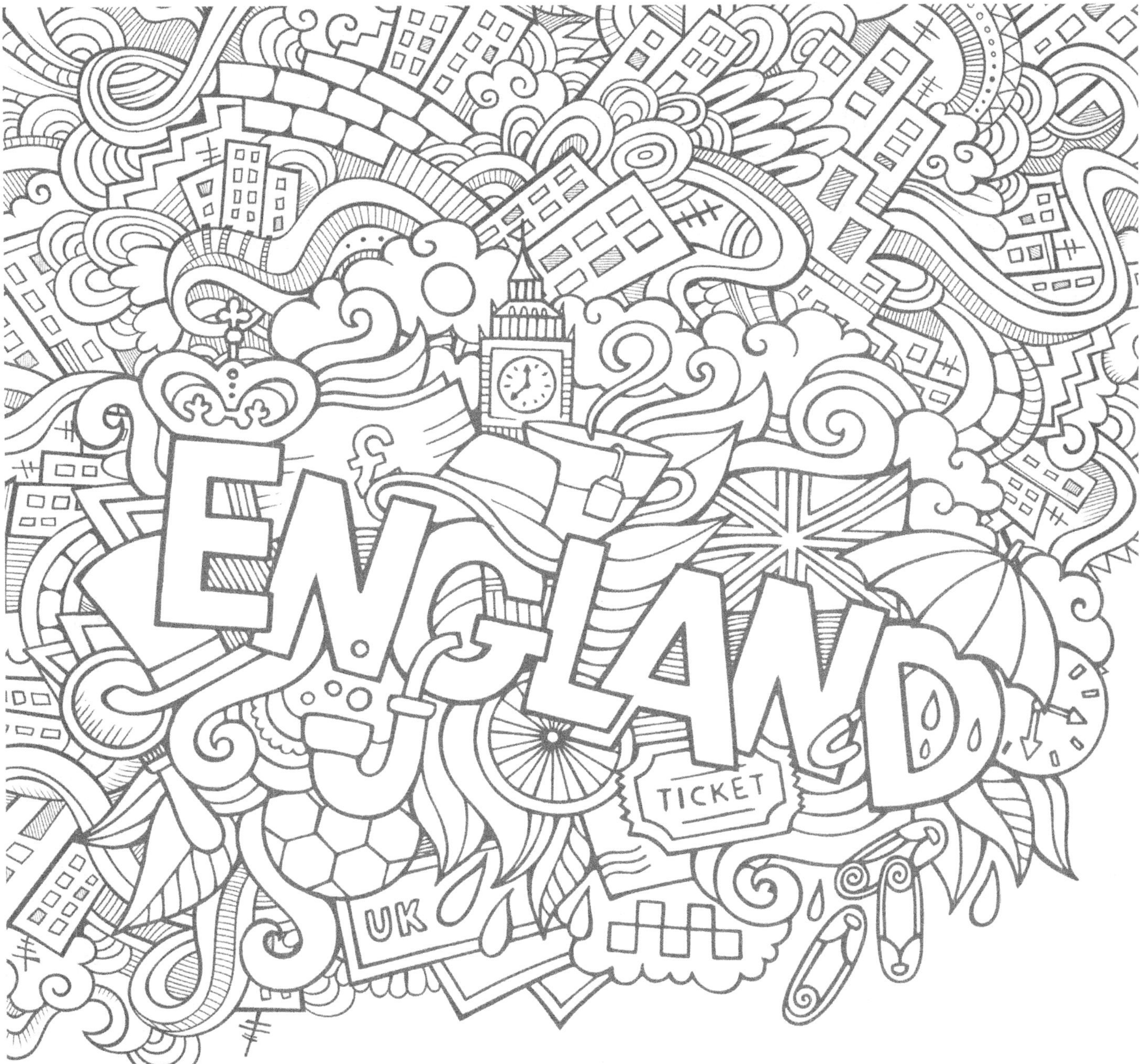
ENGLAND
TICKET
UK

NEW Coloring book at Amazon, have fun with it...

LUXURY BEDROOMS
COLORING BOOK FOR ADULTS

RACHEL MINTZ